ROLE OF MASCULINITY IN CHINUA ACHEBE'S THINGS FALL APART

DR. R. MALATHI

ISBN 979-888591062-0

Dedicated to my beloved Father Late **P. P. Rajendiran**

Contents

Preface

The book investigates the construction and representation of masculinity in Chinua Achebe's Things Fall Apart. The study digs underneath the structure and tradition of Igbo culture which celebrates the customs centered on male dominance. The protagonist, Okonkwo turns to be the major focus of study who tries to maintain all the traits of masculinity with strict application. His extreme 'macho man' life rejects any practice which might associate him with his father. The text offers the motives behind Okonkwo's sheer concern regarding preservation of male dominance. Achebe's narrative of Okonkwo's character associating description of physical power, wealth, authority and violence portrays the masculinity in Things Fall Apart. The description of wrestling, battles, yam feasts or Clan meeting upholds the supremacy of males sending all other ideals to the periphery.

Dr. R. Malathi
Dean - School of Arts and Creative Sciences
Nehru Arts and Science College
Coimbatore

Acknowledgements

I acknowledge my sincere thanks to God Almighty for blessing me to this extent. I wholeheartedly thank all my family members for their support and love.

I sincerely thank my respectful CEO & Secretary, Dr. P. Krishnakumar for his encouragement.

I am indebted to thank my beloved Principal, Dr. B. Anirudhan for his constant mentoring.

I express my gratitute to all the members of staff, Department of English for sharing hands with me in all my success.

INTRODUCTION

Literature broadly is any collection of written work, but it is also used more narrowly for writings specifically considered to be an art form, especially prose fiction, drama, and poetry. In recent centuries, the definition has expanded to include oral literature, much of which has been transcribed. Literature is a method of recording, preserving, and transmitting knowledge and entertainment. Literature, as an art form, can also include works in various non-fiction genres, such as autobiography, diaries, memoir, letters, and the essay. Within its broad definition, literature includes non-fictional books, articles or other printed information on a particular subject.

Etymologically, the term derives from Latin literatura/litteratura "learning, writing, grammar," originally "writing formed with letters," from litera/littera "letter". In spite of this, the term has also been applied to spoken or sung texts. Developments in print technology have allowed an ever-growing distribution and proliferation of written works, which now includes electronic literature. Literature is classified according to whether it is poetry, prose or drama, and such works are categorized according to historical periods, or their adherence to certain aesthetic features, or genre.

A novel is a long fictional prose narrative. In English, the term emerged from the Romance languages in the late 15th century, with the meaning of "news"; it came to indicate something new, without a distinction between fact and fiction. The romance is a closely related long prose narrative. Walter Scott defined it as "a fictitious narrative in prose or verse; the interest of which turns upon marvelous and uncommon incidents", whereas in the novel "the events are accommodated to the ordinary train of human events and the modern state of society”. Other European languages do not distinguish between Romance and novel: "a novel is le roman, der Roman, il romanzo" indicates the proximity of the forms. Although there are many historical prototypes, so-called "novels before the novel" the modern novel form emerges late in cultural history—roughly during the eighteenth century initially subject to much criticism, the novel has acquired a dominant position amongst literary forms, both popular and critically.

The publisher Melville House classifies the novella as "too short to be a novel, too long to be a short story". Publishers and literary award societies typically consider a novella to be between 17,000 and 40,000 words. Chinua Achebe (Albert Chinụalụmọgụ Achebe, 16 November 1930 – 21 March 2013) was a Nigerian novelist, poet, professor, and critic.His first novel Things Fall Apart (1958), often considered his masterpiece, is the most widely read book in modern African literature. Raised by his parents in the Igbo town of Ogidi in southeastern Nigeria, Achebe excelled at Government College Umuahia and won a scholarship to study medicine, but changed his studies to English literature at University College (now the University of Ibadan). He became fascinated with world religions and traditional African cultures, and began writing stories as a university student. After graduation, he worked for the Nigerian Broadcasting Service (NBS) and soon moved to the metropolis of Lagos. He gained worldwide attention for his novel Things Fall Apart in the late 1950s; his later novels include No Longer at Ease

(1960), Arrow of God (1964), A Man of the People (1966), and Anthills of the Savannah (1987). Achebe wrote his novels in English and defended the use of English, a "language of colonisers," in African literature. In 1975, his lecture "An Image of Africa: Racism in Conrad's Heart of Darkness" featured a criticism of Joseph Conrad as "a thoroughgoing racist;" it was later published in The Massachusetts Review amid controversy.

When the region of Biafra broke away from Nigeria in 1967, Achebe became a supporter of Biafran independence and acted as ambassador for the people of the new nation .The civil war that took place over the territory, commonly known as the Nigerian Civil War, ravaged the populace, and as starvation and violence took its toll, he appealed to the people of Europe and the Americas for aid. When the Nigerian government retook the region in 1970, he involved himself in political parties but soon resigned due to frustration over the corruption and elitism he witnessed. He lived in the United States for several years in the 1970s, and returned to the U.S. in 1990, after a car crash left him partially disabled. A titled Igbo chief himself, Achebe focuses his novels on the traditions of Igbo society, the effect of Christian influences, and the clash of Western and traditional African values during and after the colonial era. His style relies heavily on the Igbo oral tradition, and combines straightforward narration with representations of folk stories, proverbs, and oratory. He also published a large number of short stories, children's books, and essay collections. Upon Achebe's return to the United States in 1990, he began eighteen-year tenure at Bard College as the Charles P. Stevenson Professor of Languages and Literature. From 2009 until his death, he served as David and Marianna Fisher University Professor and Professor of Africana Studies at Brown University.

Achebe was born Albert Chinualumogu Achebe in the Igbo village of Ogidi on16 November 1930 to Isaiah Okafo Achebe, a teacher and an evangelist, and Janet Anaenechi Iloegbunam, a leader among church women and vegetable farmer, daughter of a blacksmith from Awka. Isaiah Achebe was the nephew of Udoh Osinyi, a leader in Ogidi with a "reputation for tolerance"; orphaned as a young man, Isaiah was an early Ogidi convert to Christianity. Achebe's parents stood at a crossroads of traditional culture and Christian influence; this made a significant impact on the children, especially Chinualumogu. Achebe's parents were converts to the Protestant Church Mission Society (CMS) in Nigeria. Isaiah Achebe stopped practicing the religion of his ancestors, but he respected its traditions. Achebe's unabbreviated name, Chinua lumogu ("May God fight on my behalf"), was a prayer for divine protection and stability. The Achebe family had five other surviving children, named in a similar fusion of traditional words relating to their new religion: Frank Okwuofu, John Chukwuemeka Ifeanyichukwu, Zinobia Uzoma, Augustine Ndubisi, and Grace Nwanneka. After the youngest daughter was born, the family moved to Isaiah Achebe's ancestral town of Ogidi, in what is now the state of Anambra.

Storytelling was a mainstay of the Igbo tradition and an integral part of the community. Achebe's mother and Sister Zinobia Uzoma told him many stories as a child, which he repeatedly requested. His education was furthered by the collages his father hung on the walls of their home, as well as almanacs and numerous books – including a prose adaptation of A Midsummer Night's Dream (c. 1590) and an Igbo version of The Pilgrim's Progress (1678). Chinua also eagerly anticipated traditional village events, like the frequent masquerade ceremonies, which he recreated later in his novels and stories.

In 1936, Achebe entered St Philips' Central School, in the Akpakaogwe region of Ogidi. Despite his protests, he spent a week in the religious class for young children, but was quickly moved to a higher class when the school's chaplain took note of his intelligence. One teacher described him as the student with the best handwriting in class, and the best reading skills. He also attended Sunday school every week and the special services held monthly, often carrying his father's bag. A controversy erupted at one such session, when apostates from the new church challenged the catechist about the tenets of Christianity. Achebe later included a scene based on this incident in Things Fall Apart (1958). As a teacher he urged his students to read extensively and be original in their work. The students did not have access to the newspapers he had read as a student, so Achebe made his own available in the classroom. He taught in Oba for four months, but when an opportunity arose in 1954 to work for the Nigerian Broadcasting Service (NBS), he left the school and moved to Lagos.

The NBS, a radio network started in 1933 by the colonial government, assigned Achebe to the Talks Department, preparing scripts for oral delivery. This helped him master the subtle nuances between written and spoken language, a skill that helped him later to write realistic dialogue. The city of Lagos also made a significant impression on him. A huge conurbation, the city teemed with recent migrants from the rural villages. Achebe revelled in the social and political activity around him and later drew upon his experiences when describing the city in his 1960 novel No Longer at Ease. While in Lagos, Achebe started work on a novel. This was challenging, since very little African fiction had been written in English, although Amos Tutuola's Palm-Wine Drinkard (1952) and Cyprian Ekwensi's People of the City (1954) were notable exceptions. While appreciating Ekwensi's work, Achebe worked hard to develop his own style, even as he pioneered the creation of the Nigerian novel itself. A visit to Nigeria by Queen Elizabeth II in 1956 brought issues of colonialism and politics to the surface, and was a significant moment for Achebe.[
Also in 1956 he was selected at the Staff School run by the British Broadcasting Corporation (BBC). His first trip outside Nigeria was an opportunity to advance his technical production skills, and to solicit feedback on his novel (which was later split into two books). In London, he met a novelist named Gilbert Phelps, to whom he offered the manuscript. Phelps responded with great enthusiasm,

asking Achebe if he could show it to his editor and publishers. Achebe declined, insisting that it needed more work African literature, literary works of the African continent. African literature consists of a body of work in different languages and various genres, ranging from oral literature to literature written in colonial languages (French, Portuguese, and English).

Oral literature, including stories, dramas, riddles, histories, myths, songs, proverbs, and other expressions, is frequently employed to educate and entertain children. Oral histories, myths, and proverbs additionally serve to remind whole communities of their ancestors' heroic deeds, their past, and the precedents for their customs and traditions. Essential to oral literature is a concern for presentation and oratory. Folktale tellers use call-response techniques. A griot (praise singer) will accompany a narrative with music. Some of the first African writings to gain attention in the West were the poignant slave narratives, such as The Interesting Narrative of the Life and Adventures of Olaudah Equiano or Gustavus Vassa, the African (1789), which described vividly the horrors of slavery and the slave trade. As Africans became literate in their own languages, they often reacted against colonial repression in their writings. Others looked to their own past for subjects. Thomas Mofolo, for example, wrote Chaka (tr. 1931), about the famous Zulu military leader, in Susuto.

The early 19th century writers from western Africa have used newspapers to air their views. Several founded newspapers that served as vehicles for expressing nascent nationalist feelings. French-speaking Africans in France, led by Lopold Senghor, were active in the negritude movement from the 1930s, along with Lon Damas and Aim Csaire, French speakers from French Guiana and Martinique. Their poetry not only Denounced colonialism, it proudly asserted the validity of the cultures that the colonials had tried to crush. After World War II, as Africans began demanding their independence, more African writers were published. Such writers as, in western Africa, Wole Soyinka, Chinua Achebe, Ousmane Sembene, Kofi Awooner, Agostinho Neto, Tchicaya u tam'si, Camera Laye, Mongo Beti, Ben Okri, and Ferdinand Oyono and, in eastern Africa, Ngugi wa Thiong'o, Okot p'Bitek, and Jacques Rabmananjara produced poetry, short stories, novels, essays, and plays. All were writing in European languages, and often they shared the same themes: the clash between indigenous and colonial cultures, condemnation of European subjugation, pride in the African past, and hope for the continent's independent future. In South Africa, the horrors of apartheid have, until the present, dominated the literature. Es'kia Mphahlele, Nadine Gordimer, Bessie Head, Dennis Brutus, J. M. Coetzee, and Miriam Tlali all reflect in varying degrees in their writings the experience of living in a racially segregated society.

Much of contemporary African literature reveals disillusionment and dissent with current events. For example, V. Y. Mudimbe in Before the Birth of the Moon (1989) explores a doomed love affair played out within a society riddled by deceit and corruption. The Zimbabwean novelist and poet Chenjerai Hove (1956-2015), wrote vividly in English and his native Shona of the hardships experienced during the struggle against British colonial rule, and later of the hopes and disappointments of life under the rule of Robert Mugabe. In Kenya Ngugi WA Thiong'o was jailed shortly after he produced a play, in Kikuyu, which was perceived as highly critical of the country's government. Apparently, what seemed most offensive about the drama was the use of songs to emphasize its messages. The weaving of music into the Kenyan's play points out another characteristic of African literature. Many writers incorporate other arts into their work and often weave oral conventions into their writing. P'Bitek structured Song of Iowino (1966) as an Acholi poem; Achebe's characters pepper their speech with proverbs in Things Fall Apart (1958). Others, such as Senegalese novelist Ousmane Sembene, have moved into films to take their message to people who cannot read.

In this culture, gender roles are strictly set for the men and women. Among the Igbo people, man rules ultimately. The more masculine one is, the higher they are respected among the community. In Things Fall Apart, Okonkwo, the main character, is one of these respected men. In order to be a man however, as the narrator states, "No matter how prosperous a man was, if he was unable to rule his women and his children (and especially his women) he was not really a man 53). With that being said, it is thought that the woman's role is to ultimately serve and be devoted to her husband. This gender role does not apply to the men of this culture, When an Igbo father gives permission for his daughter's suitor to marry her, that suitor and the men of the girl's family settle a price in which the suitor and his family pay. In the novel, Things Fall Apart, as the narrator states, "In this way Akuke's bride-price was finally settled at twenty bags of cowries" (Achebe 51). (The suitor and his family also critique the soon-to-be bride if everything goes as planned. In Things Fall Apart, the daughter of the main character Okonkwo's best friend is taking part of an arranged marriage, " Her suitor and his relatives surveyed her young body with expert eyes as if to assure themselves that she was beautiful and ripe" (Achebe 49). This ritual of marriage displays how object-like women are to the men. Igbo women gained more freedom through the new religions being brought into the country. However, there were certain expectancies of both genders in society in European culture that related back to How Igbo culture had been pre-colonization. Things like masculinity were valued among both groups, while femininity remained a female gender role, and was still not well valued among the males. In present Nigeria, women are still seen as object-like and could potentially be sold into prostitution, or used as suicide bombers. In the video, Nigeria's War against Boko Haram Claims Civilian Victims, terrorist group Boko Haram, would use female suicide bombers in attacks because of the weakness and fragility that is viewed among the female gender. Women are also being sold off into trade or being kidnapped by

MASCULINITY IN CHINUA ACHEBE'S THINGS FALL APART

The story discusses Okonkwo, the main character of the story. He is a well off man and has brought honour by tossing the amanalize the cat in a wrestling match. He had been undefeated for a very long time. He didn't care for his dad; additionally he was constantly spooky. He is a inactive man and a talented woodwind player as well. His dad unoka passed on without paying any of his obligations. After the demise of his dad Okonkwo became a clansman, rancher and family supplier.

In the social affair a speaker declares that somebody from the town of Mbaino killed the spouse of an Umofian tribesman. Group communicates their displeasure .Okonkwo is the individual who needs to convey the message that they should surrender a virgin and a young fellow. Okonkwo is the individual who addresses the family. The seniors hand over the virgin to ogbuefi udo as his better half yet they don't have the foggiest idea how to manage fifteen year old kids. Okonkwo takes the charge of the kid for protection. Okonkwo teaches his better half to deal with him .Okonkwo is an affluent man .He bolsters his three spouses and eight kids each have their own home. Okonkwo additionally has a house a stable loaded with sweet potatoes, a place of worship for his precursors. Okonkwo discovers Nwoye his child as apathetic, so he beats him continually .He fears that Nwoye additionally becomes like his father.so he generally beats him. Okonkwo assembled his fortune as a tenant farmer on the grounds that Unoka didn't have a fruitful reap. He visited the prophet he told he bombed his reap due to his sluggishness Unoka kicked the bucket due to dishonorable disease. Okonkwo needs to strive to change his dad's effect against him. He was effective in surpassing any Remaining clansman as a fighters, a rancher, family supplier .Nwakibie give Okonkwo 400 sweet potato seeds to begin a homestead. Since he was respected by Okonkwo's dedicated nature .Unoka's companion additionally gave him 400 seeds .Because of loathsome dry seasons and substantial downpour him get just a single third of the reap. Individuals who are lazier than Okonkwo didn't plant their sweet potatoes and along these lines they dodged misfortune looked by Okonkwo and other rancher's .That year's deva sting harvest left an exceptional blemish on Okonkwo.

Individuals in group designs that Ikemefuna will remain with Okonkwo. Ikemefuna is home wiped out and Nwoye's mother regards him as her own and he quickly becomes as Okonkwo's children.Ikemefuna knows numerous accounts that youngsters have never heard. He knows numerous abilities, for example, making woodwinds out of bamboo, setting snares for minimal shrubbery rodent's .He likewise become like a more seasoned sibling to Nwoye .Okonkwo didn't show any fondness towards Ikemfuna however he was found towards Ikemefuna .soon Ikemfuna calls Okonkwo as father. During the seven day stretch of harmony Okonkwo sees that his most youthful spouse Ojiugo left her cottage to have a hair meshed without planning nourishment for the supper. He beats her.

Things self-destruct shows the troublesome circumstance of an African culture. For both Okonkwo and the Umuofia society the possibility of the female is opposing and hard to support, it is simultaneously a wellspring of solace and dread, pride and disgrace. These two appearances of the ladylike in Achebe's tale are exemplified by two of the main female characters; Ekwefi Okonkwo's second spouse and Ezinma, their little girl. These two ladies shows the idea of womanhood In spite of the fact that womanhood as fused by Ekwefi and Ezinma is the most composite and enlighten vision of the ladylike in the book, the pursuer's first openness to the job of the female is through the Perspective on Okonkwo. Because of his encounters as a kid, Okonkwo has built up a short-sighted and sincerely charged perspective on ladies. This view was propelled, strangely, not by a lady but rather by a man – his dad, Unoka. Unoka was not a fruitful individual from the tribe. He didn't esteem difficult work, didn't partake in viciousness, and was substance to live off of the backs of his individual tribesmen. For breaking the feeble of harmony minister requests that okonkwo needs to charge a caretaker goat and long material and 100 cowries .Okonkwo makes amends for his transgression of breaking the powerless of harmony and follows cleric orders. After the powerless of harmony townspeople started to plan land. Nwoye and Ikemfuna help Okonkwo in planting seeds however he discovers both with their work. Ikemefuna settles with Okonkwo's family and offers the stories.

We can see the part of family connections in Achebe's Things Fall Apart a few unique ways. For one, there is the regard and landing page paid to precursors and to custom. On another level, we can notice the collaborations between our hero, Okonkwo, and different individuals from his family all through the novel. In this novel the piece of Igbo culture is offering appreciation to one's ancestors. Individuals in the general public implore the spirits of their precursors for direction, Achebe shows how significant it is in Igbo culture to respect the ancestral and to advise them on genuine matters despite the fact that they are done living. Okonkwo has to some degree stressed connections inside his own close family therefore. His oldest child Nwoye is nothing similar to Okonkwo's character; he is astute and is significantly touchier. He doesn't satisfy Okonkwo's guidelines of manliness. Oknokwo has a little girl named Ezinma with whom he is close, however his relationship with her is qualified by the way that she is female. Okonkwo has three wives, which is allowed, yet he beats one of them during the Peace Week, and that is carefully illegal. In the end, Okonkwo is banished to his homeland in the wake of Perpetrating a "female wrongdoing "inadvertently executing a man with a dose of his weapon. He isn't tolerating of his mom's clan and their point of view on sex jobs. All Okonkwo can consider is the manner by which he will return to his town and reconstruct his abundance and notoriety. Seemly, Okonkwo is an unfortunate saint since he is detached from others, including the precursors and his own family. So through Okonkwo's missteps, we may say that family connections are significant in Igbo life and on the off chance that one doesn't as expected regard those bonds, he may wind up in a difficult situation. For the Igbo, there are thoughts that structure the premise of an ideal family: shared regard for one another, veneration for every single past father, and solidarity. The dad isn't just the supplier for the family, yet protector of its honor and educator of his children. The mother's principle obligation is to add to the family line by bearing sound youngsters and furthermore to satisfy her better half. Kids are the inheritors of things to come and are raised to proceed with the estimations of the more seasoned age.

This nuclear family is the most key unit of society and its construction can be extended to fit an entire local area or even a pantheon of god. Family is significant in each culture, it shapes individuals and makes them what their identity is. Individuals are ordinarily decided by the activities of their family. Every relative contributes diversely and affects the result of their family. In various cultures the people have an assortment of jobs cut out for them, none are a remarkable same. Ladies are vital in certain societies anyway in others, for example, in the Igbo culture, they just serve to marry and bear kids. At the point when ladies are growing up one of the primary things they are instructed about is their parts in the family and future. Ladies have a vital part in picking spouses for their children in light of the fact that until the love birds can fabricate a home the wife stays with the mother by marriage at her home. This would make it vital that the relative and little girl in law get along. The ladies' primary obligations incorporate bearing solid Youngsters, satisfying their spouses and bringing up small kids. Despite the fact that ladies are viewed as the more fragile sex. Before the gathering resident's hold a banquet of New Yam to thank earth goddess Ani. Okonkwo didn't consider the gala since he considers the banquet since he thinks about them as season of inaction .Ladies enliven their hovels, expendable all unused sweet potatoes of the earlier year, use cam wood to paint their skin and youngsters with enriching plans. Okonkwo loses control and he beats his subsequent spouse. He at that point goes for chasing yet he is anything but a decent tracker. Ekwefi murmurs something out of irate; he shoots her yet misses it. After the gala the following day wrestling matches will occur. Ekwefi appreciates the challenge in light of the fact that okonkwo won her heart when he crushed the feline. Ezinma Ekwefi's lone kid takes a bowl of food to Okonkwo's hovel. He infrequently shows it. All girls bring nourishment for him.

The wrestling match happens in the town Ilo. Drummers line the field and observers are so energized. Wrestling starts with matches' young men somewhere in the range of fifteen and sixteen .Maduka child of okonkwo's companion dominates the game in no time. At the point when the wrestling match precedes Ekwefi talks with the priestess of Agbala. Because of disappointment Unoka was much of the time called an Agbala, which is a word that implies a lady or an affront that depicts a man that has taken no titles. Seeing his dad's failure to accommodate the family Okonkwo dedicated his life to difficult work and to detest all that his dad adored. Unoka's disappointments etched Okonkwo to the man he was in the novel; he turned out to be persevering and disdained sluggishness. He was the direct inverse of Unoka, acquiring numerous titles, having numerous spouses and being a fruitful man.

Chielo prophet of slopes and surrenders are the two old buddies. Ikemfuna stays with Okonkwo's family for a very long time .Okonkwo's saws such countless changes in Nwoye's conduct as a result of Ikemefuna's impact. Okonkwo as often as possible welcomes the two into his obi to tune in to savage ,manly stories , however Nwoye misses his mom's accounts, he realizes that he can satisfy his dad when his communicates his disdain for the resident's astonishment ,insect slide upon Umuofia. They come once in an age and will return each year for even a long time prior to vanishing for another lifetime.villege individuals enthusiastically gathers them since they are a great idea to eat when cooked.Ogbuefi Ezeudu visits Okonkwo yet he won't enter the hovel to share the supper. Individuals in the family educates okonkwo in private that the prophet has pronounced that Ikemefuna should be slaughtered .he advises that okonkwo not to participate in the kid's passing as Ikemefuna calls him father. Okonkwo misleads Ikemefuna that he will be getting back to his hometown .Nwoye begins sobbing uncontrollably. During the long stroll with men of Umuofia Ikemefuna felt that he will meet his mom. Twilight of strolling a man assaulted him with a weighty blade. Ikemfuna cries Okonkwo for help. Okonkwo doesn't wish to look him feeble so he cuts him. At the point when Okonkwo gets back Nwoye comprehends that his companion is dead. Something burst inside him for the second time in his life first time was newborn child crying in the malevolent woods, where new-conceived twins are left to bite the dust.

All parts of Okonkwo's life were dedicated to manliness. In any event, when cultivating he was molded by his clansmen that sweet potatoes their staple yield is the ruler of harvests. This is further the male predominance in the Ibo culture since guys will be the solitary individuals ready to accommodate the family. At the point when his family was endeavoring to give food he figured it would not be assistance since they couldn't develop sweet potatoes. He imagined that" His mom and sisters buckled down enough, yet they developed ladies' harvests, similar to coco-sweet potatoes, beans and cassava." and that "Sweet potato, the lord of yields, was a man's harvest" These accept made him look for sweet potatoes seeds at a youthful age to attempt to help develop crops for his family. Manliness is so critical to Okonkwo that he would have done all that he could to keep anybody from scrutinizing his manliness. This is because of his dad's disappointment and position in the Ibo people group. Each time he felt frail Okonkwo was helped to remember his dad's disappointment and how he couldn't accommodate his family. Which led Okonkwo to try and take an interest in the murdering of his supportive child Ikemefuna in light of the fact that "he feared being thought feeble" Afterward he dropped into a time of despondency as a result of his activities? "Okonkwo didn't taste any nourishment for two days after the passing of Ikemefuna" His perspective on manliness is high to the point that he was in any event, willing to slaughter his friends and family. One of the principle qualities of manliness that Okonkwo had confidence in was the capacity to control everybody in his family. He accepted that all individuals should submit to what he says in house and do what they were told. At whatever point any of his spouses argued or attempted to contend with him he would beat them. Okonkwo "managed his family with a substantial hand. His spouses, particularly the most youthful, lived in interminable dread of his blazing temper" likewise he accepted that "regardless of how prosperous a man was, on the off chance that he couldn't manage his ladies and his youngsters he was not actually a man" This is the reason he would consistently speak condescendingly to his kids and wives to show that he is the position figure in the house and on the off chance that anybody one would scrutinize this he would beat them.

In general Okonkwo would not acknowledge any indications of somebody testing his power as the head of his home hold. During The New Sweet potato Celebration, an Occasion that is praised by devouring a contention emerges among Okonkwo and his second spouse Ekwefi. The New Sweet potato Celebration was a period of unwinding yet according to Okonkwo it is an indication of sluggishness which he abhors so definitely. This makes him become furious and in a fit he grumbles about a banana tree which Ekwefi cut a few leaves from. "Minus any additional contention Okwonkwo gave her a sound beating and left her and her solitary girl sobbing". Okwonko turned into), an affront on his helpless chasing abilities and fired at her with his firearm. Fortunately for Ekwefi he missed, yet this demonstrated how any indication of rebellion or challenge to his manliness is unsatisfactory to him at any rate. All through the novel Okonkwo doesn't give any indications of empathy for his kids. In his point of view it is delicate and an indication of shortcoming. This is likewise the motivation behind why he never shows any adoration for his little girl Enzima. He even expressed "that he won't have a child who can't hold up his head in the social affair of the faction" and that he would prefer to "choke him with his own hands." .At one point he hastened Nyowe his oldest child and Ikemefuna his supportive child about how to develop sweet potatoes appropriately. "Deep down Okonkwo realized that the young men were still too youthful to even consider seeing completely the troublesome specialty of getting ready seed-sweet potatoes. Yet, he imagined that one couldn't start too soon. Sweet potato represented masculinity, and he who could take care of his family on sweet potatoes starting with one gravest then onto the next was an extremely incredible man in reality". This shows how significant taking care of business is and how being feminine won't go on without serious consequences in his family while he is alive. Okwonko even put his number one youngster in peril on account of his manliness. At the point when Ezinma fell wiped out Ekwefi needed to make a move, yet the Prophet would not let her.

Okwonko didn't attempt to stop the Prophet despite the fact that he adored Ezinma. He was anxious about the possibility that in the event that he showed any empathy he would be considered as to a lesser extent a man. Ekwefi couldn't make any move for the wellbeing of her own girl because it was against the practice and culture of their town Umofia. Ekwefi previously lost five different youngsters at youthful ages however since Ezinma had come to ten years old she will not allow anything to hurt her. She did all that she could to ensure her. Indeed, even before Ezinma was conceived Okonkwo recruited a medication man to help dispose of the awful soul that was frequenting her. The specialist requested that "there ought to be not any more grieving for the dead kid. At that point he removed it to cover in the Detestable Woods, holding it by the lower leg and hauling it on the ground behind him." Yet Okwonko let the Prophet remove Ezinma and just went searching for her sooner or later on the grounds that it was a masculine activity.

Okwonko's faith in the Ibo manly way of life at last leads him to his demise. He needed to make a move and murder each and every individual who was attempting to change his lifestyle that he grew up with. At the point when the couriers reached, they stopped the social event "Okonkwo drew his cleaver" and cut the lead courier down. "The courier hunched to keep away from the blow. It was futile. Okonkwo's cleaver plunged twice and the man's head lay next to his formally dressed body." At that point everybody began to frenzy and question why he executed the couriers. That was the point at which he understood his lifestyle was over in light of the fact that they let different couriers escape. Later on he ended it all by draping himself from a tree. This shows that he was so instilled in his society's way of life that when it was removed he didn't have anything left to live for. Okonkwo's acceptance of manliness led him to beat his own kids and spouse. What's more it additionally lead him to murder one of his friends and family. Despite the fact that he adored Ikemfuna like a child he abhorred shortcoming so much due to his dad's apathy and powerlessness to help his family. Okonkwo additionally accepts that sweet potatoes are the ruler of all yields like all his clansmen does in light of the fact that it is the staple harvest of the Ibo individuals of Africa. He is so instilled in the conviction of manliness that he ends it all when he found his lifestyle that he carried on with his whole life had been detracted from him. We carry on with our lives depending on the thoughts of individuals around us and when it is gone we are gone with it on account of Okonkwo.

Okonkwo surrenders to misery, he can't rest or eat. He feels frail in light of the passing of Ikemefuna. When Ezinma presents to him his evening feast three days after the fact she discloses to him that he should complete everything. He visits his companion Obierika and compliments Maduka on his effective Wrestling match.Obierika thusly demands that Okonkwo stay when his girls admirer shows up to decide a lady of the hour value .Okonkwo grumbles to Obierika that his children are not masculine enough and says that he would be more joyful if Ezinma were a kid since she has the correct soul .he and Obierika at that point squabble about whether it was right of okonkwo to participate in Ikemefuna's demise. Okonkwo's starts to feel restored to a piece .He concludes that his misery was a result of his inaction. Somebody shows up to report the passing of the most established man in an adjoining town .unusually elderly person's significant other kicked the bucket presently. Okonkwo addresses the man's evident strength once he figures out how joined he had been to his significant other.
Okonkwo sits with Obierika while Obierika deals his little girl's pride cost with the group of her admirers. After that Obierika and his future child parents in law family members talk about the varying traditions in different towns. They examine the training and ability at tapping palm trees for palm wine. Obierika discusses hearing accounts of men with skin as white as chalk. Ekwefi stirs okonkwo promptly toward the beginning of the day and reveals to him that Ezinma is biting the dust. Okonkwo discovers that Ezinma has a fever and begins gathering medication. Ezinma is Ekwefi's lone kid and the focal point of her reality. Ekwefi is lenient with her. Ezinma calls her by her first name and the dynamic of their relationship approaches correspondence. Ekwefi's nine different youngsters passed on in infancy. Okonkwo counseled a medication man who revealed to him that Ogbanje was torturing them. Ogbanje

is an insidious youngster who consistently renters its mom's belly just to pass on over and over causing its folks in .A medication man damaged the dead collection of Ekwefi's third kid to debilitate the obanjes return. At the point when Ezinma was brought into the world like most Ogbanje youngsters she endured numerous ailments; however she recuperated from every one of them. A year prior to the beginning of the novel, when Ezinma was nine a medication man named Okagbue Uyanwa discovered her Iyi – Uwa the little covered stone that is the ogbanje s physical linkmen to the soul world. Albeit the revelation of the Iyi-Uwa should have tackled Ezinma's issues, each disease that Ezinma gets still carries fear and nervousness to Ekwefi.

The town holds a stylized assembling to control equity. The tribe's genealogical spirits which are known as Egwugwu rise out of a mysterious house into which no ladies are permitted to step. The Egwugwu appear as veiled men and everybody speculates that Okonkwo is among them. The ladies and youngsters are loaded up with dread despite the fact that they sense that the Egwugwu are simply men mimicking spirits. The principal debate that precedes the Egwugwu includes a repelled couple. The spouse Uzowulu states that the three siblings of his better half, Mgbafo beat him and took her and the youngsters from his hovel however would not return her lady – cost. The lady's siblings express that he is a brutal man who beat their sister savagely, in any event, making her lose once. They contend that Uzowulu should comprehend that they will cut his private parts off on the off chance that he at any point beats her once more. The egwugwu rule for Mgbafo. One town senior gripes that a particularly silly matter ought not to be brought before them. Ekwefi reveals to her little girl Ezinma a tale about an insatiable crafty turtle. The entirety of the birds have been welcome to a dining experience in the sky and turtle convinces the birds to loan him quills to create wings so he can go to the blowout as well.as they travel to the banquet Turtle additionally convinces them to take new names for the gala too .as they travel for the banquet,

Turtle likewise convinces them to take new names for the banquet as indicated by the custom. He tells the birds that his name will be "All of you"when they show up Turtle asks his hosts for whom the gala is readied .They answer, "For every one of you." Turtle continues to eat and drink the most amazing aspects of the food and wine. The birds, irate and disappointed at getting just pieces, reclaim the quills that they had given to Turtle so he can't fly home. Turtle convinces Parrot to convey a message to his better half: he needs her to cover their compound with their delicate things so he may bounce from the sky without risk. Malignantly, Parrot discloses to Turtle's better half to draw out the entirety of the hard things. At the point when Turtle bounces, his shell breaks into pieces on sway. A medication man assembles it once more, which is the reason Turtle's shell isn't smooth.

Chielo, in her job as priestess, advises Ekwefi that Agbala, Prophet of the Slopes and Buckles, wishes to see Ezinma. Terrified, Okonkwo and Ekwefi attempt to convince Chielo to stand by until morning, however Chielo furiously reminds Okonkwo that he should not resist a divine being's will. Chielo takes Ezinma on her back and disallows anybody to follow. Ekwefi conquers her dread of heavenly discipline and follows in any case. Chielo, conveying Ezinma, gets out and about of the nine towns. At the point when Chielo at long last enters the Prophet's cavern, Ekwefi settles that on the off chance that she hears Ezinma crying she will surge in to shield her—even against a divine being.

Okonkwo frightens her when he shows up at the cavern with a blade. He quiets Ekwefi and sits with her. She recollects when she fled from her first spouse to be Okonkwo's significant other. At the point when he addressed her thumb at his entryway, they traded no words. He drove her to his bed and started to fix her attire. At first light, Chielo exits the sanctuary with Ezinma on her back. Without saying a word, she takes Ezinma to Ekwefi's cabin and takes care of her. Incidentally, Okonkwo was incredibly stressed the prior night, despite the fact that he didn't show it. He constrained himself to stand by some time prior to strolling to the Prophet's holy place. At the point when he thought that it was unfilled, he understood that Chielo was getting out and about to the nine towns, so he got back to stand by. In all, he made four excursions to and from the caverns. When he withdrew for the cavern once and for all, Okonkwo was "seriously stressed."

Okonkwo's family starts to get ready for Obierika's little girl's uri, a pledge service. The townspeople contribute food to the celebrations and Obierika purchases a tremendous goat to present to his future parents in law. The arrangements are momentarily hindered when the ladies recover a goat and the cow's proprietor pays a fine for releasing his cows on his neighbors' ranches. The admirer's relatives show up and settle the family's questions about their liberality by bringing a noteworthy fifty pots of wine to the festival. The ladies welcome the guests and the men trade stately good tidings. The gala is a triumph. Ogbuefi Ezeudu's demise is reported to the encompassing towns with the ekwe, an instrument. Okonkwo shivers. The last time Ezeudu visited him was to caution him against partaking in Ikemefuna's passing. Since Ezeudu was an incredible champion who took three of the faction's four titles, his memorial service is huge and expounding. The men beat drums and shoot their weapons. Okonkwo's weapon unintentionally goes off and executes Ezeudu's sixteen-year-old child.

Executing a clansman is a wrongdoing against the earth goddess, so Okonkwo should make amends by bringing his family into banish for a very long time. Okonkwo assembles his most significant things and takes his family to his mom's natal town, Mbanta. As indicated by the orders of custom, the men from Ezeudu's quarter consume Okonkwo's structures and murder his creatures to purge the town of his wrongdoing. Obierika addresses why a man ought to languish such a huge amount over an unplanned murdering. He at that point grieves the passings of his better half's twins, whom he had to discard, considering what wrongdoing they perpetrated.

We see Okonkwo's conduct the evening of the episode with Chielo as it appears to Ekwefi: Okonkwo appears with his blade and satisfies the job of the solid, masculine defender. The storyteller centres around Okonkwo's interior state and we see his actual sentiments as opposed to his obvious ones. Since Okonkwo sees fondness as an indication of shortcoming, he drives himself to stand by prior to following Chielo. Each time he makes the outing to the caverns and tracks down her missing, he gets back again to stand by. Not until his fourth outing does he experience Ekwefi. Okonkwo isn't simply the merciless, cutthroat man that he introduces himself to be; fairly, he is seriously stressed over Ezinma's government assistance. His exaggerated comprehension of masculinity—the aftereffect of his fatal defect—keeps his better nature from showing itself completely. Chielo's activities power Okonkwo to recognize how significant his better half and kid is to him.

The significance of connection bonds in itself shows the implications of the infringement of such bonds. At the point when Ikemefuna enters Okonkwo's family as a proxy child, he starts to mend the strain that exists among Okonkwo and Nwoye because of Okonkwo's trouble in managing the memory of his dad. Ikemefuna is along these lines introduced as a potential answer for Okonkwo's fatal defect. Yet, Okonkwo neglects to conquer his imperfection and, in murdering the kid who has become his child, harms his relationship with Nwoye for all time. Besides, he truly harms Nwoye's regard for, and adherence to, Igbo social custom.

GENDER ROLE IN CHINUA ACHEBE'S THINGS FALL APART

Things Self-destruct is to not allow pride to hinder life. Okonkwo allows his pride to impede his life and it prompts his passing. Okonkwo's pride develops from his childhood and is depicted by his activities throughout the novel. In the novel, Okonkwo is depicted as a solid, prideful, and egotistical man. HIs feelings are consistently outrageous, and his pride and haughtiness lead him to settle on sketchy choices. Okonkwo is additionally determined by his conscience and his longing to be "masculine". He thinks being a genuine man implies affirming your force and being forceful. This leads him to make moves that can be superfluous and ruinous, like murdering Ikemefuna, beating his spouses, and repudiating his oldest child. Okonkwo's relationship with his family is of finished tyranny. He is the man of the house and the top of the family who eventually runs the family. His three spouses are there to make food and bring up his youngsters. Okonkwo powers his family to work extended periods, and bothers and beats his spouses and child, Nwoye, for being "womanly". Okonkwo's pride directs the majority of his life's choices and is the explanation behind his demise toward the finish of the novel. Throughout the novel, Okonkwo is a predictable character. He continually commits vicious errors and has a reliably presumptuous mentality. Okonkwo's feeling of pride stays with him until the end. He chooses to end his own life on his own terms, as opposed to submit to the white man. For Okonkwo, giving in would make him frail and detract from his pride that is continually keeping him down. In the novel Things Self-destruct, by Chinua Achebe, the principle character, Okonkwo, has a ton of pride. There is a notable adage, Pride goes before a fall. Through Okonkwo's difficult work, he turned into an extraordinary man, with a feeling of pride and haughtiness. He at that point endured a deficiency of pride, which eventually prompted. His defeat and surprisingly his self-destruction. In this way, through Okonkwo's activities, Achebe proposes that inordinate pride can prompt destruction.

Okonkwo's uncle, Uchendu, and the remainder of his family get him energetically. They help him fabricate another compound of cottages and loan him sweet potato seeds to begin a homestead. Before long, the downpour that flags the start of the cultivating season shows up, in the strange type of gigantic drops of hail. Okonkwo buckles down on his new ranch yet with less excitement than he had the first run through around. He has worked for his entire life since he needed "to get one of the masters of the tribe," however since plausibility is no more. Uchendu sees Okonkwo's mistake yet stands by to talk with him until after his child's wedding. Okonkwo participates in the function.

The next day, Uchendu assembles his whole family, including Okonkwo. He calls attention to that quite possibly the most widely recognized names they give is Nneka, signifying "Mother is Preeminent"— a man has a place with his country and stays there when life is acceptable, yet he looks for asylum in his homeland when life is unpleasant and unforgiving. Uchendu utilizes the relationship of youngsters, who have a place with their dads however look for asylum in their moms' hovels when their dads beat them. Uchendu instructs Okonkwo to get solace with respect to the homeland appreciatively. He reminds Okonkwo that many have been more terrible off—Uchendu himself has lost everything except one of his six spouses and covered 22 youngsters. All things being equal, Uchendu tells Okonkwo, "I didn't hang myself, and I'm as yet alive.

During the second year of Okonkwo's outcast, Obierika carries a few packs of cowries to Okonkwo. He additionally brings terrible news: a town named Abame has been annihilated. It appears to be that a white man showed up in Abame on an "iron pony" (which we discover later is a bike) during the planting season. The town elderly Folks counseled their prophet, which forecasted that the white man would be trailed by others, who might carry annihilation to Abame. The residents murdered the white man and attached his bike to their consecrated tree to keep it from moving ceaselessly and telling the white man's companions. Sometime later, a gathering of white men found the bike and speculated their friend's destiny. Weeks after the fact, a gathering of men encompassed Abe's market and obliterated nearly everyone in the town. Uchendu asks Obierika what the principal white man said to the locals. Obierika answers that he didn't utter a word, or rather, he made statements that the townspeople didn't comprehend. Uchendu proclaims that Abame was stupid to execute a man who said nothing. Okonkwo concurs that the residents were fools, yet he accepts that they ought to have paid attention to the prophet's notice and outfitted themselves.

The purpose behind Obierika's visit and for the sacks of cowries that he brings to Okonkwo is business. Obierika has been selling the greatest of Okonkwo's sweet potatoes and furthermore a portion of his seed sweet potatoes. He has offered others to tenant farmers for planting. He intends to keep on presenting to Okonkwo the cash from his sweet potatoes until Okonkwo gets back to Iguedo. Two years after his first visit (and three years after Okonkwo's outcast), Obierika gets back to Mbanta. He has chosen to visit Okonkwo in light of the fact that he has seen Nwoye with a portion of the Christian preachers who have shown up. A large portion of different believers, Obierika finds, have been Efulefu, men who hold no status and who are for the most part overlooked by the group. Okonkwo won't discuss Nwoye, yet Nwoye's mom discloses to Obierika a portion of the story. The storyteller recounts the account of Nwoye's change: six preachers, headed by a white man, travel to Mbanta. The white man addresses the town through a mediator, who, we learn later, is named Mr. Kiaga. The mediator's vernacular instigates jolly giggling in light of the fact that he generally utilizes Umuofia's assertion for "my bottom" when he signifies "myself." He tells the townspeople that they are on the whole siblings and children of God. He blames them for venerating bogus lords of wood and stone. The evangelists have come, he tells his crowd, to convince the residents to leave their bogus divine beings and acknowledge the one genuine God. The residents, in any case, don't see how the Heavenly Trinity can be acknowledged as one God. They additionally can't perceive how God can have a child and not a spouse. A large number of them giggle and leave after the mediator states that Umuofia's divine beings are unequipped for doing any mischief. The teachers at that point burst into a zealous melody. Okonkwo believes that these rookies should be crazy, however Nwoye is in a split second spellbound. The "verse of the new religion" appears to respond to his inquiries regarding the passings of Ikemefuna and the twin babies, calling him "like the drops of frozen downpour dissolving on the dry sense of taste."

The missionaries demand a real estate parcel on which to construct a congregation. The town chiefs and seniors offer them a plot in the evil forest, accepting that the missionaries won't acknowledge it. To the seniors' wonder, the evangelists celebrate the offer. However, the older folks are sure that the woodland's vile spirits and powers will kill the evangelists in practically no time. Amazingly, notwithstanding, nothing occurs, and the congregation before long successes its initial three proselytes. The townspeople call attention to that occasionally their genealogical spirits will permit a culpable man an effortlessness of 28 days before they rebuff his transgressions, yet they are totally surprised when nothing occurs following 28 days. The congregation in this manner wins more believers, including a pregnant lady, Nneka. Her four past pregnancies created twins, and her better half and his family are not sorry to see her go.

One of Okonkwo's cousins sees Nwoye among the Christians and illuminates Okonkwo. At the point when Nwoye returns, Okonkwo gags him by the neck, requesting to know where he has been. Uchendu orders him to relinquish the kid. Nwoye leaves his dad's compound and goes to a school in Umuofia to master perusing and composing. Okonkwo thinks about how he might have fathered a particularly womanly, powerless child. The congregation wins numerous believers from the efulefu (titleless, useless men). At some point, a few osu, or untouchables, come to chapel. A large number of the proselytes move away from them, however they don't leave the help. Subsequently, there is a commotion, yet Mr. Kiaga immovably won't deny the pariah's participation in the congregation. He contends that they won't pass on the off chance that they trim their hair or break any of the different restrictions that have been forced upon them. Mr. Kiaga's unfaltering conviction convinces the majority of different believers not to dismiss their new confidence basically in light of the fact that the untouchables have gone along with them. The Osu before long become the most ardent individuals from the congregation. To the faction's mistrust, one flaunts that he slaughtered the sacrosanct imperial python. Okonkwo inclinates Mbanta to drive the Christians out with viciousness, yet the rulers and elderly folks choose to segregate them all things being equal. Okonkwo harshly comments that this is a "womanly" family. In the wake of declaring the new strategy of exclusion, the older folks discover that the one who bragged about slaughtering the snake has kicked the bucket of a sickness. The townspeople's trust in their divine beings is in this way reaffirmed, and they stop to exclude the proselytes.

Okonkwo's seven years of outcast in Mbanta are attracting an end. Before he gets back to Umuofia, he gives a huge banquet to his mom's family. He is appreciative to them yet furtively laments the botched chance to have additionally expanded his status and impact among his own faction. He likewise laments having invested energy with such un-manly individuals. At the blowout, one man communicates shock that Okonkwo has been so liberal with his food and other gestures of recognition of Okonkwo's Dedication to the connection security. He additionally communicates worry for the more youthful age, as Christianity is winning individuals from their families and customs.

Nwoye is attracted to Christianity since it appears to answer his since a long time ago held questions about his local religion, explicitly the deserting of twin infants and Ikemefuna's passing. Moreover, Nwoye feels himself ousted from his general public in light of his incredulity in its laws, and the congregation offers shelter to those whom society has projected out. The congregation's worth framework will permit twins to live, for instance, which offers solace to the pregnant lady who has needed to persevere through the projecting away to kick the bucket of her four arrangements of infant twins. Likewise, men without titles go to Christianity to discover attestation of their individual worth. The osu can dispose of others' impression of them as individuals from a shunned rank and enter the congregation as the equivalents of different proselytes.

Okonkwo, then again, has valid justification to dismiss Christianity. Should Mbanta not drive the evangelists away, his execution of Ikemefuna would lose part of its strict support. The harm to his relationship with Nwoye likewise appears to be more futile than previously. The two issues become his mix-up instead of the consequence of heavenly will. Besides, men of high status like Okonkwo see the congregation as a danger since it subverts the social estimation of their achievements. Their titles and their situations as strict specialists and tribe pioneers lose power and distinction if men of lower status are not there—the incredible can't be estimated against the useless if the useless have vanished.

Okonkwo has arranged since his first year estranged abroad to revamp his compound for a bigger scope. He likewise needs to take two additional spouses and get titles for his children. He has figured out how to get over Nwoye's dishonourable flight, yet he actually laments that Ezinma is a young lady. He asked that she hold on to wed in Umuofia, after his outcast, to which she assented. She even convinced her sister, Obiageli, to do likewise. Okonkwo desires to pull in interest when he gets back with two wonderful, eligible little girls.

Notwithstanding, Umuofia is highly changed following seven years. The congregation has become stronger and the white men subject the townspeople to their legal framework and rules of government. They are cruel and pompous, and Okonkwo can hardly imagine how his tribe has not driven the white men and their congregation out. Tragically, Obierika clarifies that the congregation has debilitated the ties of family relationship and that it is past the point where it is possible to drive the white men out. A significant number of the clansmen are currently on the white man's side. Okonkwo sees that the white man is exceptionally clever in light of the fact that he came in harmony and seemed to have just generous interests in the Africans, who subsequently allowed him to remain. They examine the account of Aneto, who was hanged by the public authority after he murdered a man with whom he had a question. Aneto had been unsatisfied with the new court's decision on the contest since it overlooked custom. Obierika and Okonkwo close their conversation on a fatalistic note, sitting peacefully together.

Numerous individuals of Umuofia are not totally discontent with the white man's effect on their local area. They have set up general stores, and cash is streaming into the town. Mr. Brown, the white preacher, limits his run from threatening the group. He and Akunna, one of the tribe's chiefs, meet regularly to discuss a lot of their particular strict perspectives. Akunna clarifies that the tribe additionally has only one god, Chukwu, who made the world and different divine beings. Mr Brown answers that there could be no different divine beings. He focuses on a cutting and expresses that it's anything but a divine being nevertheless a piece of wood. Akunna concurs that it is a piece of wood,

However wood made by Chukwu. Neither believers the other, yet each leaves with a more noteworthy comprehension of the other's confidence. Mr. Brown builds a medical clinic and a school. He asks the townspeople to send their youngsters to class and cautions them that on the off chance that they don't, outsiders who can peruse and compose will come to administer them. His contentions are genuinely compelling and his medical clinic wins acclaim for its therapies. At the point when Okonkwo first re-visits Umuofia, Mr Brown goes to disclose to him that Nwoye is in a trade school for instructors. Okonkwo pursues him away with dangers of brutality. Not long a while later, Mr. Brown wellbeing starts to come up short, and, pitiful, he leaves his run. Okonkwo's girls pull in numerous admirers, however to his grave dissatisfaction, his tribe takes no specific interest in his return. The ozo inception service happens just a single time in three years, implying that he should stand by two years to start his children. He profoundly laments the adjustments in his once warlike individuals.

Okonkwo's status as a hero and rancher and his group's view of him has changed since his outcast. His expanding loss of force and renown brings him extraordinary tension. Any leftover uncertainty that Okonkwo is somewhat insane is suppressed when we discover that he has been fantasizing about, and genuinely anticipating, his victorious re-visitation of his town since his flight. Okonkwo has extraordinary assumptions for himself—in Section 20 we are informed that, "he saw himself taking the most elevated title of the land." Reverend James Smith, a severe and narrow minded man, replaces Mr Brown. Man,. He requests the most extreme acquiescence to the letter of the Book of scriptures and objects to Mr Brown lenient and strange arrangements. The more passionate believers are eased to be liberated from Mr. Brown strategy of restriction. One such proselyte, Enoch, dares to expose an Egwugwu during the yearly service to respect the earth divinity, a demonstration identical to murdering a hereditary soul. The following day, the Egwugwu set Enoch's compound ablaze. They at that point accumulate before the congregation to face Reverend Smith and his kindred Christians. They tell the Christians that they just wish to annihilate the congregation to scrub their town of Enoch's loathsome sin. Smith answers that he will hold fast. He disallows them to contact the congregation, however his translator changes Smith's assertion for dread that the unvarnished truth will be too brutal and that he will endure as the courier of terrible news. He tells the Egwugwu that Smith requests that they leave the matter in his grasp. They disregard Smith's orders and consume the congregation.

Okonkwo is practically upbeat once more, notwithstanding the way that his family didn't consent to murder the Christians or drive them away. All things being equal, he and the remainder of the residents are wary, and for the following two days they arm themselves with firearms and cleavers. The Region Chief gets back from his visit and demands that the heads of Umuofia meet with him. They go, taking just their cleavers since firearms would be "improper." The official converses with them in designing terms and says that they ought to talk about the congregation's consumption "as companions." No sooner have they put their blades on the floor than a gathering of troopers shocks them. They are bound and tossed behind bars for a few days, where they endure affronts and actual maltreatment. A sort of bail is set at 200 sacks of cowries. The court couriers tell individuals of Umuofia that they should pay a fine of 200 and fifty packs of cowries or their chiefs will be hanged—by increasing the cost these couriers will make a benefit as mediators. The local announcer declares a crisis town meeting. Indeed, even Ezinma gets back from her multi day visit to her future parents in law. The following morning they choose to gather the cowries important to pay the fine.

Reverend Smith causes a lot of contention between the congregation and the tribe with his refusal to comprehend and regard conventional Igbo culture. Mr. Earthy colored, conversely, is undeniably more merciful with the believers‘ maintenance of a portion of their old convictions and doesn't draw as clear a line between the proselytes and the Igbo people group. Smith, notwithstanding, requests a total dismissal of the believers' old strict convictions. The content unexpectedly remarks that he "considers things to be highly contrasting." While from one perspective this remark alludes essentially to a powerlessness to get a handle on the degrees in a given circumstance, it additionally alludes, obviously, to race relations and frontier power. Curiously, Achebe has named Smith's archetype "Earthy colored," as though to propose that the last act of bargain and consideration is here and there identified with his capacity to see the shades between the posts of highly contrasting. Smith, conversely, is a cliché European colonialist, as the nonexclusive nature of his name reflects. His powerlessness to rehearse shared regard and resilience prompts a perilous ardent enthusiasm in a portion of the more anxious believers, like Enoch. Smith's disposition urges Enoch to affront conventional Igbo culture.

That Enoch is the child of the snake-minister makes his associated murdering with the consecrated python even more critical an offense. Enoch's change and affirmed assault on the python emblematize the progress from the old request to the new. The old religion, with its emphasis on deism and creature love, is upset from inside by one. In its place comes the new religion, which, for every one of its protestations of affection and concordance, waves a blazing rationale and furious determination to change over the Igbo at any expense. Enoch figures as a double for Okonkwo, although they espouse different beliefs. They are similar in temperament, and each man rebels against the practices and legacies of his father. Like Okonkwo, Enoch feels above all others in his tradition. He also feels contempt for them—he imagines that every sermon is "preached for the benefit of his enemies," and, in the middle of church, he gives knowing looks whenever he feels that his superiority has been affirmed. Most important, in his blind and unthinking adherence to Christianity, Enoch allows his violent desires to take over, just as Okonkwo is prone to do.

The language barrier between the colonists and the villagers enables a crucial misunderstanding to take place. Unaware of his interpreter's attempt to appease the villagers, Smith considers the burning of the church an open show of disrespect for the church and his authority. The power that the interpreter holds highlights the weaknesses and vulnerability created by the language gap, reinforcing Mr. Brown's belief that reading and writing are essential skills for the villagers if they hope to maintain their autonomy. This miscommunication reminds us of Parrot's trickiness in Ekwefi's story about Tortoise.

After their release, the prisoners return to the village with such brooding looks that the women and children from the village are afraid to greet them. The whole village is overcome with a tense and unnatural silence. Ezinma takes Okonkwo some food, and she and Obierika notice the whip marks on his back. The village crier announces another meeting for the following morning, and the clan is filled with a sense of foreboding. At sunrise, the villagers gather. Okonkwo has slept very little out of excitement and anticipation. He has thought it over and decided on a course of action to which he will stick no matter what the village decides as a whole. He takes out his war dress and assesses his smoked raffia skirt, tall feather headgear, and shield as inadequate condition. He remembers his former glories in battle and ponders that the nature of man has changed. The meeting is packed with men from all of the clan's nine villages.

The first speaker laments the damage that the white man and his church have done to the clan and bewails the desecration of the gods and ancestral spirits. He reminds the clan that it may have to spill clansman's blood if it enters into battle with the white men. In the middle of the speech, five court messengers approach the crowd. Their leader orders the meeting to end. No sooner have the words left the messenger's mouth than Okonkwo kills him with two strokes of his machete. A tumult rises in the crowd, but not the kind for which Okonkwo hopes: the villagers allow the messengers to escape and bring the meeting to a conclusion. Someone even asks why Okonkwo killed the messenger. Understanding that his clan will not go to war, Okonkwo wipes his machete free of blood and departs.

When the District Commissioner arrives at Okonkwo's compound, he finds a small group of men sitting outside. He asks for Okonkwo, and the men tell him that Okonkwo is not at home. The commissioner asks a second time, and Obierika repeats his initial answer. The commissioner starts to get angry and threatens to imprison them all if they do not cooperate. Obierika agrees to lead him to Okonkwo in return for some assistance. Although the commissioner does not understand the gist of the exchange, he follows Obierika and a group of clansmen. They proceed to a small bush behind Okonkwo's compound, where they discover Okonkwo's body dangling from a tree. He has hanged himself. Obierika explains that suicide is a grave sin and his clansmen may not touch Okonkwo's body. Though they have sent for strangers from a distant village to help take the body down, they also ask the commissioner for help. He asks why they cannot do it themselves, and they explain that his body is evil and that only strangers may touch it. No cover it, however once more, outsiders can. Obierika shows a unique blaze of temper and lashes out at the magistrate, censuring him for Okonkwo's demise and commending his companion's significance. The magistrate chooses to respect the gathering's solicitation. However, he leaves and orders his couriers to accomplish the work. As he withdraws, he compliments himself for having added to his store of information on African traditions.

The official, who is highly involved with composing a book about Africa, envisions that the conditions of Okonkwo's passing will make an intriguing section or two, if not a whole part. He has effectively picked the title: The Placation of the Crude Clans of the Lower Niger and those only strangers may touch it.

CONCLUSION

In Things Fall Apart: A Study of Gender Discrimination features and reveals the sex segregation in Igbo people group in Nigeria as it addresses the all social networks on the planet which have male controlled society as a prevailing type of sex separation. Things Fall Apart is a novel by Nigerian postcolonial creator Chinua Achebe and Igbo is a socio-social ethnic local area depicted in the novel. We find numerous normal exercises of Igbo individuals that portray and keep up the sexual orientation segregation. Both limit tops one is to venerate a lady as a divine being as Agadinwayi and the other is concealment of their status and force are found in Igbo society. Here, the attention is laid on sexual orientation jobs, manliness, gentility, socio-social status of male and female, conventional periphery of ladies and hardship of political privileges of ladies to explain a lot the sex separation in Things Fall Apart. Sexual orientation contemplates is one of the offshoots of women's activist analysis, more women's activist analysis incorporates Gender Studies as a main branch. Here it is important to make differentiation among sexual orientation and sex to under.

Okonkwo's acceptance of manliness led him to beat his own youngsters and spouse. What's more it additionally lead him to murder one of his friends and family. Despite the fact that he adored Ikemfuna like a child he detested shortcoming so much as a result of his dad's sluggishness and powerlessness to help his family.

Okonkwo additionally accepts that sweet potatoes are the ruler of all harvests like all his clansmen does in light of the fact that it is the staple yield of the Ibo individuals of Africa. He is so instilled in the conviction of manliness that he ends it all when he found his lifestyle that he carried on with his whole life had been detracted from him. We carry on with our lives depending on the thoughts of individuals around us and when it is gone we are gone withit on account of Okonkwo.

Things Fall Apart, Okonkwo is described as a persevering, valiant, forceful man. 'He has a slight stammer and at whatever point he is irate and has not got his words out rapidly enough, he will utilize his clench hands.' He has after some time become 'notable all through the nine towns and even past. His acclaim lays on strong individual accomplishments.' Not just is he referred to for his characteristics as a grappler, he has additionally 'taken two titles and has shown unfathomable ability in two between ancestral conflicts.' Moreover, he has become a well off rancher, who has quite recently hitched his third spouse. Concerning his appearance, 'he is tall and tremendous, and his thick eyebrows and wide nose give him an extremely serious look.' As such, in addition to the fact that he looks masculine with his tall, strong construction, it seems like he experiences the qualities that are seen as masculine by Ibo society. 'Military excellencies like hostility, strength, fortitude and perseverance have more than once been characterized as the characteristic and innate characteristics of masculinity.' And his greatness as a hero is by and large one of the manners by which Okonkwo affirms his masculinity. All through the novel, pursuers are helped to remember his courage. It is him who at last tosses Amalinze the Cat, a grappler unbeaten for a very long time. He is likewise the first to get back a human head won in a battle in a between ancestral conflict. Besides, he is, toward the finish of the novel, not reluctant to take on 'the white man' uniquely, if the faction neglects to wage war with him. Valiance for him is a quality so obviously and inseparably connected to manliness and the state of masculinity that 'he grieves for the warlike men of Umuofia, who have so untouchably become delicate like ladies' during the hour of his outcast. It turns out to be clear in this citation that Okonkwo asserts his masculinity, not just by practicing exercises which in his eyes are masculine, yet additionally by progressively putting himself above ladies. Ibo society, particularly like Western culture in pre-women's activist occasions, coordinates its social practice through gendered parallels. Hence, boldness, grit, animosity, movement, are completely considered to be 'manly' highlights, though, in direct resistance, shortcoming, delicacy, inactivity, and accommodation are viewed as 'female' credits. By definition at that point, 'no manliness emerges besides in an arrangement of sex relations.' 'Agbala', for example, isn't just a term for a lady, yet additionally the term for a man who is supposed to be feeble and has not taken any titles inside his group.

What's more, it is this term that definitely takes the investigation to the actual center of Okonkwo's need to affirm his manliness: his dad Unoka. In the absolute first part of the novel, it turns out to be obvious from where Okonkwo's origination of masculinity starts. In his eyes, 'Unoka, the adult, is a disappointment,' as he 'has taken no title at all and he is vigorously in the red 'when he passes on. 'Thus Okonkwo was managed by one energy – to detest all that his dad had cherished. A unique little something was tenderness and another was inaction.' all in all, Unoka, the 'Agbala', with all his character characteristics of amicability, improvidence, musicality, sluggishness, and delicacy, capacities, for Okonkwo, as a negative rendition of manliness, on which, by careful inversion, he can assemble his own, 'legitimate' idea of masculinity. His adaptation of masculinity is based, hence, on the dread of being viewed as frail. It is expressly exemplified in the manner by which he treats his child, Nwoye. Nwoye, as far as he might be concerned, is excessively 'female', like his granddad: he loves music, he reveres his mom's ethical stories and he is just excessively touchy and enthusiastic. Okonkwo feels shamed by his feminine child, considerably more so when he joins the Christian Church.

You have all seen the incredible evil entity of your sibling. Presently is not, at this point my child or your sibling. I will just have a child who is a man, who will hold his head up among my kin. On the off chance that any of you likes to be a lady, let him follow Nwoye now while I'm alive so I can revile him. In the event that you betray me when I'm dead I will visit you and break your neck.'
Once more, there is the gendered separation among shortcoming and ladies, and strength and men. Manliness is, for Okonkwo consistently affirmed by this gendered, twofold resistance. 'Men close to ladies are binded to the sexual orientation designs they have inherited,'W and Okonkwo is by all accounts mindful of this, as he utilizes this development to nearly 'power' his different children into carrying on masculine. Okonkwo devotes himself to being just about as many as could be expected, and through his ascent to turn into an influential man of his clan and ensuing fall both inside the clan and according to his child Nwoye, the novel investigates the possibility of manliness. Okonkwo trusts in customary sex jobs, and it torments him that his child Nwoye isn't more forceful as is he. Therefore, it's noteworthy that he communicates the wish that his girl Ezinma was a kid—from this we realize how affectionate he is of her. Furthermore, in a gathering towards the earliest reference point of the book, Okonkwo affronts a man without title by considering him a lady, exhibiting how much manliness is esteemed when positioning those in Umuofia society. At last, however, Okonkwo's adherence to manliness and animosity prompts his fall in the public arena—he gets fragile and unfit to twist with the progressions occurring in his family. With regards to this guideline of manliness, Okonkwo compels himself to execute his own substitute child, murder the white man contrary to what he would usually prefer, and drape himself before a discipline can be forced by others. Okonkwo's animosity makes him powerless

Eventually. It leaves him with no space to move against the more inconspicuous methods of the white man.

Nwoye battles with this thought of manliness, as he needs to satisfy his dad by being forceful and customary, at the end of the day, he's repulsed by the viciousness in Umuofia ceremonies and joins the Christians. Nwoye's flight can likewise be connected to this thought from Okonkwo's uncle, Uchendu, after the family is banished from Umuofia: "'the facts demonstrate that a youngster has a place with its dad. Yet, when a dad beats his youngster, it looks for compassion in its mom's hovel.'" Similarly, subsequent to being beaten by his dad, Nwoye leaves to look for comfort in the more female and apparently delicate Christian religion.

References

Achebe, Chinua. 1959. Things Fall Apart. New York: Doubleday Anchor.

Adebayo, Tunju, The Past and the Present in Chinua Achebe's Novels. The African studies, 1974

Bhaba, K. Homi. The Other Question: Difference Discrimination and the Discourse of Colonialism, in out There Marginalization and Contemporary Cultures, Cambridge, 1992.

Beier, Ulli. Introduction of African Literature, Longman, London, 1979.

Boon, K. A. (2005). "Heroes, Metanarratives and the Paradox of Masculinity in
Contemporary Western Culture." The Journal of Men's Studies. 13. 3. pp: 301+. Men's Studies Press. 2005

Cook, David. African Literature: A Critical View, Longman, Harlow, 1985.

Echeruo, M.J.O. Chinua Achebe, A Celebration of Black and African Writing. ed. Bruce
King and Kolawole Ogunbeasan, Zarie and Ibadan : Ahmadu Bello University Press and Oxford University Press, 1975.

Eddah W. Chinua Achebe and Tradition, Standpoints on African Literature A Critical Anthology, (ed.), Chris, L., London, 1980

Fischer, A. R., & Good, G. E. (1998). "New directions for the study of gender role Attitudes: A cluster analytic investigation of masculinity ideologies." Psychology of Women Quarterly, 22, 371-384.

Gerard, Albert. African Language Literatures, Longman, London, 1981.

Glenn, Ian. Achebe and the Dilemma of the Nigerian Intellectual, London, 1990

Helgeson, V. S. (1994). Prototypes and dimensions of masculinity and

femininity. Sex Roles, 31, 653-682.
Kubayanda. Josaphat. 1987. "Things Fall Apart: Viewers Guide:' Department of Romance Languages and Literatures. Ohio State University.
Larson, R., Charles. The Emergence of African Fiction, 1971, Macmillan, London 1971.
Murrie, L. (1998). Changing Masculinities: Disruption and Anxiety in Contemporary Australian Writing. Journal of Australian Studies. 2002.
Obiechina, Emmanuel. Culture. Tradition and Society in the West African Novel, Cambridge University Press, 1975.
Ohaeto. Ezenwa. 1997. Chinua Achebe: A Biography. Bloomington and Indianapolis: Indiana University Press.
Stratton. Florence. 1994. Contemporary African Literature and the Politics. London: Rutledge.

9 798885 910620

Printed by Libri Plureos GmbH in Hamburg,
Germany